ISBN 978-1-330-11179-6
PIBN 10028567

1 MONTH OF
FREE
READING

at

www.ForgottenBooks.com

By purchasing this book you are eligible for one month membership to ForgottenBooks.com, giving you unlimited access to our entire collection of over 1,000,000 titles via our web site and mobile apps.

To claim your free month visit:

www.forgottenbooks.com/free28567

English
Français
Deutsche
Italiano
Español
Português

www.forgottenbooks.com

Mythology Photography **Fiction**
Fishing Christianity **Art** Cooking
Essays Buddhism Freemasonry
Medicine **Biology** Music **Ancient**
Egypt Evolution Carpentry Physics
Dance Geology **Mathematics** Fitness
Shakespeare **Folklore** Yoga Marketing
Confidence Immortality Biographies
Poetry **Psychology** Witchcraft
Electronics Chemistry History **Law**
Accounting **Philosophy** Anthropology
Alchemy Drama Quantum Mechanics
Atheism Sexual Health **Ancient History**
Entrepreneurship Languages Sport
Paleontology Needlework Islam
Metaphysics Investment Archaeology
Parenting Statistics Criminology
Motivational

AT LAST,

A Temperance Drama,

IN THREE ACTS,

——BY——

Geo. S. Vautrot, Esq.

AUTHOR OF

The False Friend, Nigger vs Yankee, etc.,

to which is added
a description of Costume, Characters, Entrances and Exits, and the whole
of the Stage business, Correctly printed from the Auth-
thor's approved Copy.

—:×:×:—

Entered according to Act of Congress in the year 1879, by
A. D. AMES,
In the office of the Librarian of Congress, at Washington.

—·◇·❮❯·◇·—

——CLYDE, O:——
A. D. AMES. PUBLISHER.

AT LAST.

CHARACTERS.

Frank Montgomery...A wealthy young farmer.
Charles Scranton..A gambler.
Bill Morgan..his Confederate.
Moses...colored servant of Montgomery's.
Thomas Wren..A detective.
Eli Perkins..An old fashioned man.
Hans Christopher....................... ....keeper of the "Grape Vine."
Ruth Montgomery...................Frank's wife, and daughter of Eli Perkins.

—

TIME—Soon after the war of the rebellion.

—

Costume, Modern, to suit station and character, except Moses. His first
dress to be very ragged, dirty etc., with a large sack thrown over his
shoulder, his make-up, that of a street rag-picker. Second dress, neat.

—

SCENE—Mobile, Alabama.

— **TMP92-007454**

TIME OF PERFORMANCE—one hour and thirty minutes.

AT LAST.

ACT I.

SCENE FIRST—*Royal street—first grooves—the sign "Grape Vine" prominent—enter Scranton, L., whistling, and toying with his watch chain, in a careless manner at c.—looks down the street—whistles very loud—whistle is answered—lights a cigar, as he does so Morgan enters L., smoking.*

Scran. Howd'y do, Bill, feeling well this morning?

Mor. (*yawns*) Why. yes, I believe I do.

Scran. Havn't seen any thing of Wren, have you?

Mor. No, that is not since last night.

Scran. Wish I could see him.

Mor. If I see him, I'll make it a point to tell him that you wish to see him.

Scran. I'd be much obliged to you, Bill, if you would.

Mor. Do you wish to see him particularly?

Scran. No.

Mor. If you did, why, I would say that you would not have long to wait, for as the old saying is, "speak of the devil and—"

Enter Wren, R.

Wren. Good morning, gentlemen.

Scran. { Good morning.
Mor. {

Wren. Rather cool this morning.

Mor. Yes, rather chilly.

Wren. Let's have a drink.

Scran. Just what I was about to propose.

Mor. I'm agreeable.

Wren. Come on then.   (*exeunt* R.—*scene changes to*

SCENE SECOND—*Interior of the Grape Vine—table with four chairs around it, R.—ditto, L.—Hans behind counter, R., wiping glasses and smoking a huge pipe.*

Hans. Mine gootnsss alive, what ish der matter mit der fellers in dis town, anyhow? I vash coomed here tinkin' I vas makes my fortune, und 1 don't make so much as my meat. Dey vas told me, dem rebs vas drink like a camel; but I don't can see why dey vas say so. Dey don't coom here, I vonder vats der matter?

Enter Scranton, Morgan and Wren, R.

How you vas, shentlemen. (*flies around smartly*) Vat can I do for der shentlemens dis morning. (*Scranton and party seat themselves at table, R.*

Mor. Here old lager-head, bring us a bottle of wine, and be quick about it, I'm as dry as—

Hans. Now you big fools, look here, I yoost tole you dat my name ish not lauger-head; but Hans Christopher.

Mor. Why, you infer—

Hans. Und if you vas call me oud from my name, I vas yoost throw you der sidewalk oud.

Mor. You infernal saur-kraut eating dutch hog, I'll squeeze the life out of you, if——

Scran. (*lays hand on Morgan's arm*) Oh, come, Bill, dry up. What's the use of raising a row with dutchy, when we've business on hand?

Wren. Yes, that's what I say. It wouldn't be much of an honor to .put a head on dutchy.   (*winks at Hans*

Hans. Vell, ven you vas got ready to put vun head on me, got yerself ready at der same dime to tote a gouble of heads, yourself.

Wren. Hush up, Hans, he didn't mean to insult you.

Hans. If dot ish so, it's all right.

Scran. Well, where is the bottle of wine?

Hans. In vun minute, shentlemens. (*takes bottle of wine from shelf—takes tray with wine and glasses to party*) If yer wants anything else shentlemens, yoost call, und if I vas haf it, you shall haf it. (*goes behind counter—wipes glasses—watches party as though afraid they were trying to beat him*)

Mor. (*filling glasses*) Well boys, I hope this wine is as good as it looks.

Scran. It is good. I've been here before.

Wren. So have I.

Mor. (*raises glass*) Here's luck to everything that either of us three undertake. (*all drink—shouts of "stumps, stumps," outside*) Here dutchy, how much?

Hans. Ein dollyer und a half.

Mor. Here's your money.   (*Hans takes money—shouts repeated*

Hans. Vot ish dem noises out door for?.

Scran. Oh, nothing, only a nigger rag picker, that the news-boys are in the habit of hollowing at.

Mor. Well, boys, let's be going.

Wren. We'll call again, dutchy.

Hans. I vill be most happy to see you shentlemans. (*make motions as if bidding him good-bye—exeunt* R.—*scene changes to*)

SCENE THIRD—*Same as scene first—shouts of "stumps, stumps" and laughter, outside—enter Moses* R., *in first dress.*

Moses. You're good for nuffin, low down white rebel trash. Yer ain't good for nuffin, but ter holler at 'spectable gemmen in de street. Don't spec yer knows I'm a duke, in disguise, jest a gwine 'round de world.

(*shakes stick off wing,* R.—*shouts repeated—starts after them—stops—picks up piece of paper—shouts repeated from time to time—muttering to himself—is angry—pulls off coat, and places it on sack*)

I ain't a gwine to stan' dis foolishness no longer, I ain't. I'm a gwine ter kotch one ob dem boys, I is, an' when I does kotch him, why—— (*spits on hand—shakes stick—exit* R.

Enter boy, L.—*hides coat and sack,* L. 3 E.—*exit* L.—*enter Moses,* R.

Dem boys kin run de fastest ob.any boys I eber did see. 'Tain't no use; run as fast as yer kin, ye can't kotch 'em. Wonder wot time is it. I done brung my watch down to de foundry, to get a wheel made, an' dey ain't got it done yet, so I'll hab ter—— (*misses things—excitedly*) Whar dat coat? Whar dat sack? (*prancing around furiousnly*). Show me de man wot stole dat coat—de best coat I ebber had. I'll bust his snoot, I will. (*cries*) If anybody'll show me whar dat coat is I'll give 'em five cents. I knows w'at I'll do. I'll go an' git a p'liceman. Dem de fellers w'at'll fetch em.   (*exit* L.—*scene changes to*

SCÉNE FOURTH—*Parlor at Battle House, elegantly furnished—Scranton sitting at fireplace,* L., *reading a paper, looks at watch.*

Scran. Wonder, what in the name of goodness, keeps Mr. Montgomery. It is now over five minutes since I sent my card to him. So he is the one whom my pretty little Ruth prefered to myself. Wonder if she will recognize me now. If she does, my little game will be checked ; but I must trust to luck and Bill Morgan.

Enter Frank Montgomery, C.

Frank. (*advances and shakes hands with Scranton*) · Glad to see you, old fellow, am sorry that I kept you waiting so long, but my wife, she——

Scran. Oh yes, I understand, a young wife on her honeymoon trip doesn't like to have her husband out of her sight, eh, old boy ?

Frank. Well, no, not exactly that ; but this is the first time she has ever been to a city, and it is the first time I ever was in Mobile, myself, so you see she is naturally nervous.

Scran. By the way, Frank, I would like very much to become acquainted with your wife.

Frank. And you shall, my dear fellow, at the first oportunity ; but how did you know I was stopping here ?

Scran. Oh, the papers told me that.

Frank. True, I had forgotten.

Scran. Don't drink, do you ?

Frank. Very seldom, thank you.

Scran. Some other time, then.

Frank. I tell you what, Charlie, I'd like to take a look around the city. Are there any sights to be seen ?

Scran. (*aside*) The very thing. (*aloud*) Well, I should think there were !

Frank. When will you be at leisure ?

Scran. I will initiate you to-night, it you say so.

Frank. Let it be to-night. then. Where will I meet you ?

Scran. Any place you like

Frank. Say the post office.

Scran. All right, so good day, old fellow, and I promise you lots of fun to-night. (*shake hands—exit* L.

Enter Ruth, C.—*sees Scranton—stares at him—pause—music.*

Ruth. Who is that man, Frank ?

Frank. (*starts at the sound of her voice*) Why, Ruth, darling, is it you ? What was it you said.

Ruth. I asked who that man was.

Frank. His name is Charles Scranton. Why do you ask ?

Ruth. I thought I recognized him.

Frank. It must have been a resemblance to some one.

Ruth. Perhaps it was. (*loud and confused noise outside—they look out of window and laugh*) I declare, that's the funniest I ever saw.

Frank. Well, he is a character. (*calls*) Here boy. (*shakes head—points —nods head*) We'll have him up here presently.

Ruth. Dear me, how comical.

Frank. It was, and as I am in need of a servant, what do you say to hiring him ?

Ruth. If you think him capable and trustworthy, why suit yourself.

Enter Mose L. *cautiously—looks at room in amazement.*

Mose. Great land ob Sodom !

Frank. Here, boy. (*Moses starts to run*) Come here.

Mose. I wa'n't doin' nuffin, Boss.

Ruth. Don't be frightened—we won't hurt you.

Mose. Missis, I declare ter goodness, my bref like ter left my body.

Ruth. How was that?

Mose. I neber, in all my borned days seed de likes ob dis room. Is you de queen ob England?

Ruth. No—what makes you ask?

Mose. Kase I—kase yer—kase der—— Oh, lordy! (*starts to run*)

Frank. Come back. What is your name?

Mose. I'm de chil wot were found in de rushes.

Frank. Ha, ha ha! Good! Well, what made you turn black?

Mose. Well, yer see, boss, while I was a lying dar, a bull rushed at me, flipped me ober in de mud, de mud dried outer me, an' it neber comed off, see?

Frank. Yes, how would you like to be my servant?

Mose. Wat, wait on yer an' der young missus dar?

Ruth. Yes, Moses, my husband is in need of a servant.

Mose. I'm de huckleberry fer yer pie.

Frank. All right, come with me and I will see if we can't get you some better clothes.

Mose. Dese here is good enough, boss, I've been wearin' 'em for four years, and dey ain't worn out yit.

Ruth. Go with Frank, Moses, and do as he says.

Mose. All right, missis, I's agreeable.

Frank. Come on then, as I wish to get back in time for dinner.

Mose. (*aside, rubbing his stomach*) Dinner—dat's de time o' day I likes to hear 'em talk about.

Frank. Good bye, darling. I'll be back presently.

Ruth. Good bye, Frank.

Mose. Good bye, missus. I'll take good care ob him.

(*exit Frank and Mose, c.*

Ruth. I feel—I know—but can it be possible? If it really is Lieutenant Harry Forbes, whom I refused during the war, on account of his being a gambler and a drunkard—if it really is him under the assumed name of Scranton, whom I saw speaking to my husband in this room, he is meditating harm to Frank, for he swore vengeance against me and mine. I'll watch him as a cat does a mouse. (*exit, c.—scene closes*

———

SCENE FIFTH—*Dauphin street.—2d grooves.*

Enter Frank and Mose, r.

Frank. Well, I think we can get what we want in that store yonder.

Mose. Anywhar you say, boss.

Frank. Come on then. (*they enter one of the stores l.—as they go in*

Enter Wren, r.

Wren. It seems to me that everything ain't square about that fellow Scranton and his pard. I'll watch 'em however, and if they kick up any of their didos, I'll jug 'em. (*goes up stage*

Enter Scranton and Morgan, l. 1 e.

Mor. Which way did he go?

Scran. He went into that store. (*points l.*

Mor. We will wait until he comes out. You say you know him well?

Scran. Yes.

Mor. Then he's our meat—but how about his wife?

Scran. Leave her to me; I don't think she recognizes me.

Mor. Then the game is safe?

Scran. Yes, if that infernal detect——

Mor. Hu-s-h, there he is now. (*seeing him*

Scran. (*sees Wren who is slowly coming down* C.) I'll cook his goose if he interferes.

Mor. Good enough. (*Wren walks slowly forward, head bowed as if in deep thought*) I say Wren, you don't seem to know your friends.

Wren. (*looking up*) Ah, good morning gentlemen. (*aside*) I hope I shall be forgiven for that.

Scran. We were just speaking of you.

Wren. Saying anything good about me?

Mor. Why, of course we were.

Wren. Then I won't demand satisfaction. (*all laugh*

Scran. Pistols and coffee for six.

Wren. Meet me by moonlight alone.

Mor. Wait till the clock strikes nine.

Scran. That'll do boys. (*signs to Morgan*

Mor. Have something, Wren?

Wren. Don't care if I do.

Mor. (*to Scranton*) Ta, ta, old boy—see you to-night.

Scran. All right. (*Morgan and Wren lock arms and exit* L.) I don't half like the way that detective hangs around—but then if he's in any way troublesome, why over he goes. Halloa—just look.

Enter Frank and Mose from the store, L. *Mose has on new clothes.*

Scran. (L.) He must have hired that nigger for a servant—must get on the right side of him. (L. C.—*to Frank*) How are you Frank?

Frank. (R. C.) Why, Charlie, how goes it?

Scran. Been hiring a new servant?

Frank. Yes. What do you think of him?

Scran. I think he's a likely lad, and bound to suit you.

Mose. (*aside*) I knows yer, ole hoss—can't soft soap dis nigger.

Scran. Which way, Frank?

Frank. Back to the hotel for dinner.

Scran. All right. I'll see you again.

Frank. Yes, I'll not forget. (*exit Scranton* L.

Mose. (R. C.) Look heah, Marse Frank, dat's de worstest kind ob a man, he is.

Frank. Hush up. Don't let me ever hear you say a word against any of my friends again.

Mose. (*aside*) You'll find out before you's done wid him dat he's de worstest frien' dat you eber had.

Frank. Come on—we'll be going. (*they start off* R. *Mose struts about behind his master. As they exit, scene changes to*

SCENE SIXTH.—*Royal street, first groovs.*—*Frank enters* R., *stands by a lamp-poast.*

Frank. I wonder how long I'll have to wait—I hope not long, for I do detest waiting for any one.

Enter Scranton and Morgan, L.

Scran. Hallo, Frank, at your post I see.

Frank. Yes.

Mor. Been waiting long?

Frank. No.

Scran. Come on, let's be traveling.
Frank. All right.   (*they exit* L.

Enter Wren, R.

Wren. I must watch those two chaps, that young fellow will fall an easy victim to them I fear. I think I know the lay they are on, so here goes.   (*follows them off* L.

SCENE SEVENTH.—*Same as scene fourth.*—*Ruth is discovered sitting on sofa,* R.

Ruth. Oh, dear! but three weeks married, and he can leave me here alone, and at night. He said that he had an engagement with Mr. Scranton—Mr. Scranton—(*she shudders*) oh, what a dread that man's face brings to my heart—I saw him as he passed this afternoon—He looks like Harry Forbes—it must be—yes, it is him, and he meditates harm to Frank—What can I do?—I have it.   (*rings bell.*

Enter Mose, C.

Mose. (C.) Here I is Missus. Kin I do anything fer ye?
Ruth. Moses, did you see your master leave in company with another gentleman?
Mose. Yes'm I did, an' I seed 'em takin' a drink down stairs.
Ruth. (*aside*) This confirms my suspicions—Frank cannot stand much liquor. (*aloud*) Moses, do you follow them—mind I do not wish you to play the spy; I would scorn the action, but I am afraid that some harm is meditated to your master, from that man. Here, go—go!   (*gives him money.*
Mose. (*takes money, puts it in his pocket—clenches his fist—raises his hand up very slowly—looks straight at Ruth*) Gwine ter hurt Massa Frank, is he—ef he teches Massa Frank, I jest double myself up an' I'll butt him, an' ef he don't gin up de ghost, yer kin kick me round fer a foot ball. Hi, golly, I jess want ter see 'em hurt massa Frank, I does.   (*exit* C. *quickly.*
Ruth. Oh, dear me, I wish that I had never induced Frank to come to the city; it was all on my account that he came; but now that we are here—Oh, I hope Frank will not get into trouble, because if he does, I don't know what I would——(*a pistol shot is fired outside*—*Ruth runs to sofa, throws herself on it, hides her face in her hands—and scene closes.*)

SCENE EIGHTH.—*Same as scene first.*—*Frank, Scranton and Morgan enter* L. *Frank seems to be slightly intoxicated.*

Frank. I say boys, where'll we go now?
Scran. Let's go and play keno.
Mor. No, let's get another drink.
Frank. All right, let's go over to the Grape Vine—eh?
Scran. Come on then.   (*they exit* R.

Enter Mose L.

Mose. I knowed it, I knowed it—dey'se done got massa Frank toxicated, and now dey'se gwine ter mu'der and den rob him. But dey shan't do it —shan't do it, not when dis nigger's round.

He hitches up his pants, buttons up his coat very determinedly, takes a chew of tobacco and follows the party—as 'he goes off Wren crosses behind him—a pistol shot is heard, L.—*the whole party rush in* R. *Frank in the lead, he is very drunk.*

AT LAST.

Frank. Where's the—hic—row? What's the—hic—matter, eh?
Mose. (*goes up to Frank*) Come along wid me massa Frank, and go home.
Frank. Go to the—hic—devil.
Mose. You'se wid de debbil's brudder now.
Ssran. What's that you say? you black imp of satan.
                                    (*starts towards him.*
Mose. Come on, and I'll bet yer a free cent stamp you'll git hurt.
Mar. (*catches hold of Scranton*) Hold on Charley.
Scran. Oh, I'm right here!
Mose. You won't be dar long, ef yer fool wid dis chap.
Wren. You had better go home with your servant, Mr. Montgomery.
Frank. You—hic—think so—hic—eh?
Wren. Yes I think so.
Frank. Come on—hic—Mose, this—hic—gemmen—hic—thinks I'd—hic—besser go—hic—home.
Mose. Come on den boss.
        (*he catches Frank by the arm and leads him off* L., *the others follow.*

———

SCENE NINTH.—*Battle house, parlors as before, Ruth sitting at table with book in her hand—lamp on table—distant clock strikes two—Ruth starts, looks nervously around, shuts up book, is very agitated.*

Ruth. Two o'clock, and not returned yet—I cannot sleep—Oh, where is my husband?—How can he stay away from me? and in that man's company. But he does not know him—no, no, no—Frank is too noble, too generous to suspect anyone—ah, what was that? (*Frank in a loud and unsteady voice singing,* "We won't go home till morning.") It is as I feared; Frank has returned, and he is intoxicated.
            (*rises, looks towards door with her hands clasped—soft music.*

Enter Frank supported by Mose, L.

Frank. Hallo, ole—hic—girl, ain't gone to—hic—bed yet?—hic—didn't I tell you not to sit up for—hic—me—hic—eh? (*Mose tries to drag him out*) Hol' on—hic—Mose, I—hic—know what I—hic—am about, don't I ole—hic—gal?
Ruth. Oh, Frank, Frank!   (*throws herself on sofa and sobs violently.*
Mose. Come, Massa Frank, come, go to bed.
Frank. (*loud and boistrously*) I—hic—won't do—hic—it, I'm—hic—banged if I—hic—do.
Ruth. (*rises from sofa, goes up to Frank, puts her arms around his neck*) Please don't make such a noise, Frank you'll wake up all the people.
Frank. Who the—hic—devil cares if I—hic—do, eh?
Ruth. I do, Frank.
Frank. (*furiously*) You—hic—do eh? Then take that! (*pushes her violently—she reels and falls on the sofa—Frank is sobered instantly—starts towards her.*)

QUICK CURTAIN.

ACT II.

SCENE FIRST.—*Scranton's rooms, nicely furnished—table in center, de-canter on it; also glasses and several packs of cards—Scranton discovered seated* R., *Morgan* L., *both are smoking cigars—Scranton fills Morgan's glass.*

Scran. Here's luck old pard. (*they drink*) If it hadn't been for that in-fernal nigger, we would have had everything to suit ourselves.

Mor. Yes, curse him, and I would have been better off by three or four hundred dollars.

Scran. If I thought—well, never mind, we'll fix him yet.

Mor. How do you propose to work?

Scran. I intend to get him on another spree; after he is rather full, in-vite him up here, propose a game of cards—and of course you know the rest?

Mor. Of course I do. But I am afraid it will be hard to manage this detective.

Scran. Oh, no! I'll fix him.

Mor. How?

Scran. Get him to drink, and then drug him.

Mor. Won't that be dangerous?

Scran. Not in the least.

Mor. Perhaps he will not be around.

Scran. So much the better.

Mor. How soon do you intend to put your plan into operation?

Scran. At the very first opportunity.

Mor. Then I'll keep on the watch.

Scran. I wish you would, for there is no telling at what moment I'll want your assistance.

Mor. All right, old pard; count me there every time.

Scran. Well, I must go down town, as I have some business to attend to.

Mor. Think I'll vamose the ranch too.

Scran. All right, we'll go together.

Mor. Just as you say.

Scran. Have another drink before you go?

Mor. Sling her out.

(*Scranton fills glasses, they clink, then drink, and exit* L.—*scene closes.*

SCENE SECOND.—*Royal street as before.*

Enter Mose, L., *smoking, his looks very dandified.*

Mose. Jess tink, here I is, got good close, good chuck good place ter stay, bully young boss, an' de sweetest kind ob a young missis; an' not long ago I neber had nowhar ter sleep, nuffin ter eat, an' no money. Hi, golly! beliebe I'll go down ter de tair ternight an' make er mash. Oh, go 'long Lizer Jane!

Enter Wren, L.

Howdy do, Massa Wren!

Wren. Frigates, Mose.

Mose. Dey ain't no free gates 'round here, massa Wren.

Wren. Then come over and have a free lunch.

Mose. I'm yer persimmon, boss.

Wren. See here Mose, you haven't seen anything of those two fellows who were with your master the other night, have you?

Mose. No sah, I has not, an' I'm gwine ter keep my eye peeled fer 'em, yer kin bet yer socks.

Wren. Watch them close, and mind your eye.

Mose. Dis nigger wan't raised in de gutter fer nuffin, he wasn't.
Wren. How did Mr. Montgomery get over his spree?
Mose. He's de sickest man you eber did see.
Wren. What! he isn't sick yet?
Mose. Yes sah! he's got de distemper.
Wren. What?
Mose. Dey's sunfin de matter wid his head.
Wren. So long? Mose, I must be going.
Mose. So long, massa Wren. (*exit Wren.* R.) wonder whar dat free lunch is—spec it's ober dar yet. Hi, golly! de young missus gib me ten dollars ter buy a pistil wid, an' here it am. (*takes a small pistol from his pocket, looks at it admiringly, cocks it and is unable to put the hammer down*) How de debbil's I gwine ter git dis here ting down? (*tries again, and in doing so discharges the pistol—falls to floor, screaming*) I'm dead, I'm dead, send for de doctor, send for everybody!

Enter Wren, R.—*runs up to Mose and shakes him.*

Oh! I'm dead, I'm dead! I sees de angels coming arter me, I does!
(*Wren catches him by the collar and puts him on his feet.*
Wren. Here, you're not hurt at all.
Mose. Yes I is, massa Wren, de bullet went clar frough my skull. I seed all de little stars, and comets, and all dem tings.
Wren. Where did it hit you?
Mose. Right here boss.
(*puts his hand on forehead—Wren looks and takes the bullet off.*
Wren. Here's the bullet, mashed as flat as a pancake.
Mose. (*looks bewildered*) Hanged if eber I thought dis nigger's head was so tough. (*takes bullet*) I'm gwine ter wear dat on my watch chain. Look here, massa Wren, I ain't no free lunch stricken, I ain't.
Wren. (*aside*) Loud hint, very. (*aloud*) Come on Mose.
Mose. (*aside*) Thought dat would fetch him. (*they exit* L.

SCENE THIRD.—*Battle house parlor as before—Ruth sitting by fireplace.*

Ruth. Oh, my poor husband, I fear he is in terrible peril, for let strong drink once master a man of his impulsive nature, it is hard to drive the demon away. And I, a poor weak woman, what can I do? Oh! would to heaven that we had never come to this accursed city. But it was my wish, and Frank has never denied me anything. I must have a confidant; my husband must, and shall be saved.

Enter Frank, C.—*Looks weary and tired out.*

Good morning, husband.
Frank. Good morning, Ruth. (*aside*) No word of reproach, this is more than I can bear.
Ruth. (*approaches him, lays her hand on his shoulder, looks into his face*) Are you not well this morning, dear?
Frank. Yes, dear Ruth, quite well. (*he turns his face aside.*
Ruth. I wish you would make me a promise.
Frank. Best of wives; I know what you wish me to promise, and I give you my word that I'll not drink any more.
Ruth. (*puts her arms around his neck*) Thanks, dear husband, and may God help you to keep your promise.

Enter Mose C.—*sees how matters are, retreats rapidly—Ruth releases Frank and calls.*

Mose! Mose!

Enter Mose, **c.**

Mose.   Here I is, missus.

Ruth.   Did you do as I bid you?

Mose.   Yes'm, and here am de effects ob de first fire.

(gives the flattened bullet to Ruth.

Ruth.   Why, what is this?

Mose.   Here am de facts ob de case: Dat's a bullet, dat is, an' dat bullet tried ter find out which was de hardest, it or dis nigga's head.

Ruth.   What do you mean?

Mose.   Dis here's what I mean. I got dat ar little tool, an' I was 'zam'ing it, when de blamed fing went off an' hit me in de head.

Ruth.   Did it hurt you?

Mose.   Oh, no! it didn't hurt. I only seed sebenteen millin's shootin' stars, sky rockets, nigger chasers, nineteen fourth of Julys before de war, and one StPatrick's day frowed in, all to-gedder at de same time. Oh, no! it nebber hurt!

Ruth.   But how did you come to get the bullet?

Mose.   I reached up ter see if de whole top ob my head was blowed off, and dar stuck de bullet flat up agin de skull.

Ruth.   Your head must be hard, indeed.

Mose.   You kin jest bet yer, and——

Frank.   What was it you were about to say, Mose?

Mose.   I was about to say, if you wanted dese yere walls butted down, gimme de job, dat's all.

Frank.   Come Mose, let's go out and see those trunks we were looking at.

Mose.   All right, boss.

Frank.   By—by—Ruth, we'll be back in the course of an hour or so.

Ruth.   Don't be gone long, Frank, it's so lonesome without you.

Frank.   No, I won't be gone long.

As he gets to c. *door turns and kisses his hand to her—Mose follows him—as he gets to the door.*

Ruth.   Mose.

Mose.   Yes'm.   *(comes back.*

Ruth.   Don't let him drink, Mose.

Mose.   No'm, I won't, *(aside)* if he don't ax me.

Ruth.   That's a good boy. here's something for you.   *(gives him money.*

Mose.   Much obliged, ma'am.

Frank.   *(outside)* Mose! Mose!

Mose.   Yes sah, I'se comin.'   *(runs out* c.

Ruth.   I fear—what? I don't know myself; but every time my husband leaves me, an indiscribable fear takes possesion of me; what shall I do? I have it—I'll write to father; I'll feel safe when he is beside me, I'll do it this very instant. *(seats herself at table and prepares to write.—scene closes.*

SCENE FOURTH.—*Royal street.*

Enter Frank and Mose, **R.**

Frank.   Want to smoke, Mose?

Mose.   Yes sah.

Frank.   Run down to that cigar store and get a couple of the best cigars they have.   *(hands Mose money.*

Mose.   All right, boss.   *(runs off* L.

Frank.   That's a cute nigger, puts me in mind of one I used to own during the war; if anybody knew how to keep his mouth shut and his eyes open he did.

Enter Scranton, L.

Scran. How goes it, old boy?

Frank. First rate, I thank you, and how is it with yourself?

Scran. So, so! feel kinder loose this morning, believe a good drink would set me all right though, have something?

Frank. I would, only I promised my wife that I would not touch another drop.

Scran. Bah, man, one drink won't hurt you, so come on.

Frank. I know it, but then I——

Scran. Oh, come on, take some soda.

Frank. All right, I will. (*they exit* R.

Enter Mose, L., *smoking.*

Mose. Whar de debbil is massa Frank done gone to? Don't see him no whar, bet a nickle he sent me off so he could go and get a drink. I'm bound to follow him. (*exit* R.

SCENE FIFTH.—*The Grape Vine as before.—Hans behind the counter.*

Enter Frank and Scranton, R.

Hans. How you vas, shentlemens?

Scran. Oh, first-rate—fix me up a whisky cock-tail.

Frank. Give me soda.

Scran. Put a stick in it Hans.

Hans looks at Frank, he does not understand, Hans seems satisfied, and proceeds to mix the drinks.

Enter Morgan, R.

Mor. Well, well, how goes it fellows.

Scran. Here, landlord, another cock-tail.

Mor. Not for me. I want mine straight.

Hans. All right.

He places the two drinks, one before Frank and one before Scranton, then a black bottle and glass before Morgan, then three glasses of water. They clink glasses and then drink.

Frank. Look here, Hans, I asked for soda.

Hans. Yah, dot vas so, und your friend says, "put a stick in it,"—you nefer says nothings, und now you vas growling.

Scran. Is it possible, old boy, you didn't understand me?

Frank. Oh, it's all right.

Mor. What do you say to a quiet game of cards.

Scran. I'm agreed.

Frank. (*hesitatingly*) Well, I'll play a couple of games.

They seat themselves at table R.—*Hans brings a pack of cards—Frank* R. *Morgan* C. *Scranton* L.—*Mose enters, looks round—goes up to table.*

Hans. See here, you black rascal, I don't can stand de fifteen commandment.

Frank. That's all right, Hans, he's my servant.

Mose. (*aside to Frank*) See here massa Frank, better git out ob dis.

Scran. What shall we play?

Frank. Euchre is my best hold.

Scran. All right then, euchre it shall be.

Mor. I'll be game keeper.

Mose. (*aside*) An' I'll be de watcher.

*They play—the cock-tail begins to tell on Frank—Scranton and Morgan ex-
change glances. Frank looks at Hans and snaps his finger, Hans brings a
bottle of wine and glasses, places them on table—Mose turns around and his
elbow strikes the bottle, it falls off the table—Scranton jumps up and starts
at him—Mose jumps back and draws his pistol—Scranton stops—Hans
comes behind him and knocks the pistol from his hand—Scranton starts at
him again, Frank jumps up with a chair in his hand.*

Frank.   The first one that touches that nigger, I'll brain him.
Mose.   (*grasps a chair and gets by Frank*) Here we is, de bofe ob us.
Scran.   Come, come, Frank, old boy, don't get mad.
Mose.   Whar's dot dutchman what hit me? (*turns, sees Hans*) Oh! dar
you is. (*starts at Hans, who retreats, cries out "Police! Police!" scene closes.*

SCENE SIXTH.—*Royal street as before.*

Enter Frank, Scranton and Morgan, R. *they are very jolly—Frank especially.*

Scran.   What do you say Frank, let's go up to my rooms?
Frank.   All right—good enough.
Scran.   I say Morgan, go and get a box of cigars, will you?
Mor.   I'm yours to command.
Scran.   Very well, go down to Peter Burke. He keeps the best cigars
in town.
Frank.   (*catches hold of Scranton*) Oh, come on, if you're coming!
Scran.   Easy, old boy, don't tear my clothes.
Frank.   Well, then, come on.
Scran.   Don't be so impatient.
Frank.   Let's sing.
Scran.   No.
Frank.   Why not?
Scran.   People will think we are tight.
Frank.   I don't care if they do, I'm going to sing—so here goes.
            (*commences to sing—Scranton takes hold of him and takes him off,* L.

Enter Mose and Wren, R.

Wren.   Where is your master, Mose?
Mose.   He's find dem two fellers, agin.
Wren.   I'm afraid he's in bad company.
Mose.   In bad company, he's in de wustest kind ob company.
Wren.   Hallo, who's that old gentlemen coming down the street?
Mose.   How's I gwine ter tell, seeing as I has neber seed him afore?
Wren.   I'll bet ten dollars he's from the country.
Mose.   You's hit it dat time, massa Wren.
Wren.   I'm going to chin him.
Mose.   Better not.
Wren.   Why?
Mose.   See dat stick?
Wren.   Yes.
Mose.   Well, look good at dat stick, dat's all I'se got ter say.
Wren.   Believe I'll take the hint.

Enter Eli Perkins, R.—*huge stick in one hand, carpet bag in the other.*

Per.   Good-day, gentlemen!   (*Mose grins at being called a gentleman*
Wren.   Same to you sir.
Per.   Kin you tell me whar my darter is?
Wren.   If I knew her name, perhaps I could.
Per.   That's so, that's so! her name is Ruth—Ruth Perkins that was,
but now Ruth Montgomery that is, she married ole Judge Montgomery's
son.

Mose. An' his fust name am Frank.

Per. You've struck it, young man.

Mose. Den I'm de one kin show yer whar she am.

Per. Kin you neow, sartin shure?

Wren. Yes, sir, he can, he is in the employ of Mr. Montgomery.

Per. Du tell!

Mose. Come on Mister Perkins, dinner'll——

Per. Heow in the world did you know my name was Perkins?

Mose. Yer tole me dat yer darter's name was Perkins, an' I kinder thort dat her daddy's name orter be de same—un'stan?

Per. Neow, you is smart.

Mose. Let's hurry, kase dinner am mighty nigh ready.

Per. All right, come on.

Mose. Here, gimme dat sarpet-kack.

(*Mose takes carpet-bag, exit with Perkins* L.

Wren. I feel confident that Scranton is trying to injure young Montgomery, but what can I do? the law does not reach their cases—I'll watch, and leave no means untried to save him from these scoundrels. (*exit* L.

SCENE SEVENTH.—*Scranton's rooms as before.*

Enter Frank and Scranton, C.

Scran. Well, old boy, what do you think of my bachelor apartments?

Frank. Why, I'm astonished.

Scran. I thought you would be; take a seat. (*Frank sits* R. *of table, Scranton opposite*) Have a drink?

Frank, Well, I don't care if I do. (*Scranton pours liquor in glasses—they drink*) That's prime old port.

Scran. You can gamble heavy on that. Talking about gambling, what do you say to a quiet game?

Frank. I'm agreeable.

(*Scranton takes a pack of cards, shuffles them, deals out hands, they play*

Enter Morgan C., *with cigars—he comes to table.*

Mor. Amusing yourselves, eh?

Scran. Yes, have a game?

Mor. No, I do not care to play.

Scran. Take a cigar, Frank.

All three take cigars, they light and commence to smoke—Frank wins first game. He seems elated. Scranton fills glasses again, they drink, play again, Frank wins the second time. He is very much excited—they drink again.

Frank. Say, Charlie, old boy, believe I could beat you playing poker.

Scran. You think so?

Frank. I do.

Mor. Then play.

Frank. I'll do it.

Mor. How much ante?

Scran. Say one dollar.

Frank. Good enough.

(*the liquor tells on him—Scranton gets another pack of cards.*

Scran. (*starting to deal*) Are you playing, Morgan?

Mor. Yes, I'll try one or two hands, if I don't win.

Frank. Let 'em slide, Charlie.

Scranton deals—Frank looks at his hand, lays it on table, rubs his hands—Morgan picks up his hand, looks at it, throws it down with disgust—Scranton picks his up, doesn't seem to like it, but still he plays.

Scran. Well, Frank, what is your hand worth?
Frank. Fifty dollars.
Scran. I see that, and go you one hundred better.

They go on in this way till the pot reaches the sum of five hundred dollars—then

Scran. Show your hand. (*Frank shows, and wins—they take another drink. Same business a second time*) Well, here goes for the last time, then we'll quit.

·*Frank.* All right.   (*Mose pokes his head in door* c.
Mose. (*aside*) Oh, ho! dar you is.   (*he watches.*

Scranton deals out hands—Frank holds four kings—Morgan throws his hand down with a curse—Scranton holds a small hand, but reaches down in his pocket and brings up four aces—Mose sees the movement, shakes his fist at Scranton—Frank and Scranton commence to bet, when the pot has reached the sum of one thousand dollars, Scranton calls him—Frank shows four kings and is about to rake in the pile, when Scranton shows four aces—and,

Scran. Not so fast Mr. Montgomery.
Mose. (*jumps forward*) Not so fast Mr. Scranton. (*he levels pistol at him—Montgomery attempts to get up, but staggers, he finally succeeds*) I·seed you pull dem four aces outer yer pocket, I did.

Scranton jumps at Mose, who pulls trigger, the pistol snaps—Scranton knocks Mose down—Frank pulls his pistol, it goes off accidentally, shoots Morgan; he screams, throws up his hands and falls—Frank is horrified, and completely sobered—Mose jumps up, runs to Frank, lays his hand on his arm, this arouses him, he gives one look at Morgan, and starts to run Scranton cries, "police—help." Just as Mose and Frank get to c. *door, he shoots at them, Mose returns the fire—Scranton staggers—as he falls—*

QUICK CURTAIN.

ACT III.

SCENE FIRST.—*Parlor at Battle House, as before.*

Enter Perkins, c., *smoking a corn-cob pipe.*

Per. Darter tole me not ter smoke in these here rooms, but I don't see how that's a goin' tew hurt 'em; then she said it wan't aristocratic to smoke in here. Well, I'm a going tew dew it anyhow, fer I never enjoy my victuals unless I have a good smoke, and (*looks round and places his hand to his mouth*) a good drink of old Jamaica rum—I tell you what——

Enter Ruth, c.

Ruth. Ah, father dear. (*Perkins hides his pipe, it burns his fingers, he makes wry faces*) You've been smoking.
Per. No, I haint, darter.
Ruth. But I smell the tobacco.
Per. Oh, that comes from the street.
Ruth. Have you seen Frank yet?
Per. No, I have not; where in the world is he?
Ruth. I don't know. (*dejectedly*) Oh! I feel certain that man has accomplished his ruin. He was out all night.
Per. Yeow don't say so?
Ruth. Yes, he and Mose were together.
Per. Well, I'll go and hunt him up.
Ruth. I wish you would.
Per. Yeow jest let the old man alone; he knows a thing or two.

Ruth. I hope you will find him.

Per. I'm bound tew. (*exit* c.

Ruth. Where is my husband? I shudder to think what has befallen him—Oh, Frank, Frank, if you knew the misery that your conduct has caused me to endure, I am certain you would never break the promise you have made me—but you have a tempter. Ah! well did I know the man who pretended to be your friend—he is now having his revenge. Be still, fluttering heart—there is a way to save him, and that way must, and shall be found, if it should cost me my very life—for I will never——

Enter Mose, c.

Mose. Drink any more.

Ruth. (*turns, startled, and sees Mose*) Where is your master?

Mose. I dunno, missus.

Ruth. You don't know?

Mose. No, ma'am, no more an' you does.

Ruth. (*alarmed*) Tell me, Mose, what has happened?

Mose. Dey'se dun bin a heaps ob tings happened.

Ruth. Tell me quick, where is Frank?

Mose. Well, I'll commence at de fust startin' pint, and den I'll get it straight.

Ruth. Go on, go on. (*aside*) I am so frightened, I hardly know what to do.

Mose. Well den, fust and foremost, to begin at de beginnin', der right place ter start, I shall proceed to unfold myself—unstan'?

Ruth. Do go on!

Mose. Dat's what I'm a doin'. I'se a gwine on.

Ruth. Do tell me what has happened?

Mose. Gib me time ter think an' I will.

Ruth. (*sits* R. *of table*) I'm all patience. Proceed.

Mose. I hasn't got ter der perceedings yet. I'll get ter dem arter awhile. (*Ruth waves her hand for him to go on*) Well den, as I said before, ter commence at de beginnin'. You know when I left de hotel? (*Ruth bows her head*) You does? den de story am commenced——

Ruth. Mose! Mose! for God's sake tell me the worst, and——

Mose. I ain't got no worst ter tell yer.

Ruth. (*aside*) I feel a dreadful presentiment of evil, and Mose is trying to prepare me for it—faithful fellow.

Mose. Den arter us had left de hotel, we went down de street—massa Frank axed me if I didn't want ter smoke, ob course I tole him yes. He gibbed me some money an' tole me ter get two ob de bestest cigars I could find. Den I went arter dem cigars, an' when I come back, massa Frank wasn't dar.

Ruth. Where was he?

Mose. Hold on, hold on! I'll get dar presently, bimeby. As I said, he wasn't dar—I looked all round, couldn't see him nowhar—den here comes massa Wren——

Ruth. Who?

Mose. massa Wren.

Ruth. Who is he?

Mose. He's one ob dem detectin' chaps.

Ruth. Detecting chaps?

Mose. Yes ma'am, he catches thieves and de likes.

Ruth. Yes, I see, he is a detective.

Mose. Dat's it missus—you'se a cute un, you is—arter I seed massa Wren, I axed him whar massa Frank done went ter—he didn't know, but 'spected he'd gone wid Mister Scranton, kase he'd seed him coming dat way.

Ruth. (*aside*) It is as I thought—that man has prevailed upon him to drink again.

Mose. Jest as soon as I heard dat, I started for de fust bar room, kase I knowed dar's whar I'd find massa Frank—an' sure enuff dar he was playing keards wid Mister Scranton an' anuther villain—dey was tryin' ter get him drunk, so's ter make him lose his money, but I were too sharp for 'em.

Ruth. How did you prevent it?

Mose. (*laughs softly*) Massa Frank called for a bottle ob wine—an' I got up close ter der table, an' I went ter turn 'round, I hit de bottle wid my elbow and——

Ruth. Knocked it off the table?

Mose. Dar's whar you's right missus. (*aside*) Golly, she's a cute un. (*aloud*) De bottle hit de floor—an' dat bottle was defunct, played out, busted all ter pieces—Mr. Scranton got mad, jumped up ter hit me—I pulled my persuader onto him, an' he kinder reconsidered de original movement —de dutch bar-keeper knocked de pistol outer my hand—an' Mister Scranton come at me again—massa Frank jumped up wid a chair in his hand, an' said dat de fust man wat hit me was a gwine ter get hurt——

Ruth. And was there a fight?

Mose. No ma'am, not dat time, de fightin', an' shootin', an' cuttin' cum in arterwards.

Ruth. (*lays her hand on her heart*) Oh, heavens!

Mose. Soon's massa Frank jumped up, I made for de dutchman, an' he commenced to holler for der police, an' I run——

Ruth. Well, what next?

Mose. De next ting, am meetin' de ole boss, an' fetchin' him here, an'—

Ruth. I know all about that. Proceed.

Mose. An' right here am where de proceedin's am comin' in. Here am whar dis nigga seed trials an' tribulations.

Ruth. Mose do not keep me in suspense—what happened next?

Mose. I went ter look for massa Frank agin—didn't know more'n a fool whar ter look. I commenced ter think—a idea struck me—didn't hit me so hard as dat bullet did.

Rtth. What was that idea?

Mose. De idea was, dat massa Frank has done gone wid dem chaps ter dar rooms, an' I were kirect. I found de place, an' dar dey was playin' keards—I seed massa Frank was tight. Den I seed Mister Scranton drop some ob his keerds, an take four from his pocket. Massa Frank had a good hand an' he bet five milyin dollars on it—dey showed der' hands, and de Mister Scranton wanted der money—I tole massa Frank how it was. Mister Scranton come at me, an' I pulled on him—Massa Frank got out his pistol, an' it went off axidently an' shot de odder feller. Me an' massa Frank started out, an' Mister Scranton drawed his pistol an' shot at massa——

Ruth. (*jumps up excitedly*) I knew it! I knew it! Frank is shot—Oh, God in heaven, give me strength to bear this cross.

> (*covers her face with her hands, and sinks into chair.*

Mose. Spec' you's a gittin' too fast, missus—massa Frank ain't hurt.

Ruth. (*runs to Mose, lays her hands on his arm*) Not hurt, did you say? Not hurt?

Mose. No ma'am, he neber teched him.

Ruth. Oh, joy, joy! Heaven be praised, my husband is unharmed.

Mose. Yes ma'am, but de odder feller ain't.

Ruth. How?

Mose. Well, nuffin much, only he didn't hab time ter do nuffin.

Ruth. What do you mean?

Mose. I means dat as soon as he fired dat pistol at massa Frank, dis nigga's right hand went up—an' dat right hand had a pistol in it, an' somehow dat pistol shot dat feller, dat's all.

Ruth. This is terrible.

Mose. Yes, I should think it was fer dem two fellers, any how.

Ruth. But where is Frank?

Mose. He'll be 'round here 'fore long.

Ruth. Mose, you shall be handsomely rewarded for your fidelity to my husband.

Mose. I nebber gibbea massa Frank any fi—fi—fi—what was dat you said missus?

Ruth. I meant for the way you stood by your master.

Mose. (*very impressively*) See here, missus Ruth, I ain't nuffin but a poor niggar. I knows I ain't much account, but when a white man stands by me like massa Frank did, I'm a gwine ter stand by him as long as dar's wool on de top ob my head, dat's de kind ob box ob blackin' I is.

Enter Frank and Perkins c. Frank seems very much worn out—passes his hand across his forehead several times—walks down stage—Ruth sees him.

Ruth. (*runs to him, puts her arm around his neck*) Oh, Frank! Frank!

Lays her head on his breast, sobs. Frank is terribly moved—raises her head, gently—kisses her forehead—disengages himself from her—drops on one knee.

Frank. Listen Ruth, thou noblest of God's creatures. (*raises his right hand to heaven*) Oh, God, with your help, and the help of my noble and suffering wife, I swear never again to touch a drop of this accursed liquor, in any manner, shape, or form.

Ruth. (*drops on her knees, beside him, lifts her eyes to heaven*) Oh, heavenly Father, I thank thee for this, give my husband strength to resist this perilous temptation.

Per. Amen.

Mose. De angel ob de house hab conquered. Glory hallelujah.

MOSE.   PERKINS.

R.   FRANK.   RUTH.   L.

All kneeling.

CURTAIN.

16. *THE SERF.* A Tragedy, in five acts. by R. Talbot Esq.. 6 males, 3 female characters. Good parts for 1st and 2nd Tragedian, and Tragic lady. The character of Ossip is very powerfully drawn. The history of his early love—of his marriage—the indignities he is made to suffer, and the death of his wife, is highly wrought; and his sarcastic levity and deep revenge are unfolded with a terrible earnestness. Scene, apartments in castle. Time about 2 hours and a half.

17. *HINTS ON ELOCUTION AND HOW TO BECOME AN ACTOR.* This valuable work has just been published, and contains valuable instructions that amateur actors, and every one that ever expect to make a favorable appearance in public, cannot do without it. It teaches you how to become a good and efficient reader, reciter, debater, a good actor, how to hold an audience silent, and treats on every subject that is necessary to be acquired in order to become a good and pleasing actor.

18. *THE POACHER'S DOOM.* A Drama in 3 acts, curtailed and arranged by A. D. Ames, 8 male, and 3 female characters. A thrilling drama, always a favorite. Leading man, villian, two comedies, old man, leading lady, comedy lady, etc. Costumes modern. The situations in this play, are most excellent. Time of performance, 1 hour and a half.

19. *DID I DREAM IT?* A Farce in one act by J. P. Wooler. 4 male, 3 female characters. Scene, drawing room. The question "Did I Dream it" is what the farce is founded upon. Very strange things happen, and a nice little love scrape helps to color the plot. A good piece. Costumes simple. Time of performance 45 minutes.

20. *A TICKET OF LEAVE.* A Farce in one act, by Watts Phillips, 3 male, 2 female characters. A play written by this author is sufficient guarantee of its excellence. Scene, a sitting room, plain furniture. Costumes modern. Time of performance, 35 minutes. This is an excellent farce.

21. *A ROMANTIC ATTACHMENT.* A Comedietta in one act, by Arthur Wood, 3 male, 3 female characters. A most excellent little play, well adapted for school exhibitions, lodges, amatuers, etc. The scenery is simple, being a plain room, is always a favorite with every company which plays it. Time of performance, 35 minutes.

22. *CAPTAIN SMITH.* A Farce in one act, by E. Berrie, 3 male, 3 female characters. This excellent little farce is equally well adapted for school exhibitions, etc., as No. 21. The dialogue is sparkling, not a dull speech from beginning to end. The plot simple, the piece easily performed. Scene, a plain room. Costumes modern. Time of performance, 30 minutes.

23. *MY HEART'S IN THE HIGHLANDS.* A Farce in one act, by William Brough and Andrew Halliday, 4 male, 3 female characters. Scene, exterior of house in the Highlands. Costumes, simple Highland. This farce is easily produced and very effective is full of fun, caused by the mishaps of two characters, who go from the city to the country, and do not know a pig from a roebuck, nor a turkey from an ostrich. Time of performance, 25 minutes.

24. *HANDY ANDY.* An Ethiopean Farce in one act, 2 male characters. Scene, a kitchen. Costumes, exagerated and comic. The difficulties in procuring a good and suitable servant are most ludicrously set forth in this farce. Time of performance, 20 minutes.

25. *SPORT WITH A SPORTSMAN.* An Ethiopean Farce, in one act, 2 male characters. Costumes, exagerated sportsman's dress, and boyish dress. Scene, a wood. Time of representation, 20 minutes. A tip top negro farce.

26. *THE HUNTER OF THE ALPS.* A Drama in one act, by William Dimond, 9 male, 4 female characters. Scene in-door and forest. Costumes, Swiss. Rosalvi, the hunter of the Alps leaves his home to procure provisions to keep his wife and children from starving, meets Felix, a lord, and demands, and finally implores of him money. Felix moved with compassion gives him money, and goes with him to his hut, and there discovers they are brothers. There is some fine comedy in it. The story is beautifully told. Time of performance 1 hour.

27. *FETTER LANE TO GRAVESEND.* An Ethiopean Farce in one act, 2 male characters. Scene, plain room. Costume, exagerated and comic. The two characters, Ike and Hystericks are very funny, and will keep an audience in roars of laughter. Short, easily produced, and a tip top farce. Time of performance 15 minutes.

28. *THIRTY-THREE NEXT BIRTHDAY.* A Farce in one act, by John Madison Morton, 4 male, 2 female characters. Scene, outside of hotel, easily arranged. Costumes to suit the characters. This farce should be read to be appreciated, and is a good one as are all of Madison Morton's plays. The comedy characters are excellent. Time of performance, 35 minutes.

29. *THE PAINTER OF GHENT.* A Play in one act, by Douglass Jerrold, 5 male, 2 female characters. Scene in Ghent. Costumes of the country and period. This is a beautiful play of the tragic order. The character of the "Painter of Ghent" is one of grandeur and fine language. He becomes insane at the loss of children, and being a painter, paints their portraits from memory. A daughter whom he supposes dead, returns to him, and he recovers. A grand pley. Time of pertormance, 1 hour.

30. *A DAY WELL SPENT.* A Farce in one act, by John Oxenford, 7 male, 5 female characters. Scenery simple. Costumes, modern. Two clerks in the absence of their "boss" conclude to shut up shop, and have a spree. They get into several scrapes with the females, have numerous hair breadth escapes, and have a terrible time generally. Very amusing. Time of performance, 40 minutes.

31. *A PET OF THE PUBLIC.* A Farce in one act, by Edward Sterling, 4 male, 2 female characters. Scene, parlor. Costumes, modern. In this farce, the lady assumes four distinct characters, either of which is good. For an actress of versatility, it is a splendid piece, and amatuers can also produce it without troubi. It can either be used for a principal piece, or an afterpiece. Time of perform lice, 50 minutes.

32. *MY WIFE'S RELATIONS.* A Comedietta, in one act, by Walter Gordon, 4 mal 4 female characters. Scene, plain apartments. Costumes, modern. A pleasing little piece well suited to amatuers, school exhibitions, etc. A fellow marries, her relatives comes to see her, are much more numerous than he has an idea of. The denoument is funny. Time of performance, 45 minutes.

33. *ON THE SLY.* A Farce in one act, by John Madison Morton, 3 male, 2 female characters. Scene, plain apartment. Costumes, modern. Husbanos, don't never fall in love with your wife's dress makers—never squander your money foolishly, never do anything "on the sly," for your wives will be sure to find it out. This farce explains it all. Time of performance 45 minutes.

34. *THE MISTLETOE BOUGH.* A Melo Drama in two acts, by Charles Somerset, 7 male, 3 female characters. Scene, castle, chamber and wood. Costumes, doublets, trunks, etc. A most excellent Melo-Drama. Plenty of blood and thunder, with enough jolly, rollicking fun to nicely balance it. A great favorite with amatuers. Time of performance 1 hour and 30 minutes.

35. *HOW STOUT YOU'RE GETTING.* A Farce in one act, by John Madison Morton, 5 male, 2 female characters. Costumes, modern. Scene, a plain room. This is another of Morton's excellent farces. The comedy characters in it are nicely drawn, and it always is a favorite. Easily produced. Time of performance, 35 minutes.

36. *THE MILLER OF DERWENT WATER.* A Drama in three acts, by Edward Fitzball, 5 male, 2 female characters. Costumes, modern. Scenery, easily arranged. This is a touching little domestic drama, abounding in fine speeches, and appeals to the better feelings of one's nature. The "Miller" is an excellent old man. Two comedy characters keep the audience in good humor. Time of performance, 1 hour and 30 minutes.

37. *NOT SO BAD AFTER ALL.* A Comedy, in 3 acts, by Wybert Reeve 6 male, 5 female characters. Costumes, modern. Scenery, simple and easily arranged. Every character in this comedy is in itself a leading character, and every one very funny. Probably there is not a play in the language in which every character is so funny as this. Time of performance, 1 hour 40 minutes.

38. *THE BEWITCHED CLOSET.* A Sketch in one act, by Hattie Lena Lambla, 5 male, 2 female characters. Scene, Parson Grime's kitchen. Costumes modern. A lover goes to see his sweetheart, hides in a closet. Old man appears on the scene, thinks the closet bewitched. They upset it. Old man is frightened—runs away. Everything right etc. Time of performance, 15 minutes.

39. *A LIFE'S REVENGE.* A Drama in 3 acts, by Wm. E. Suter, 7 males, 5 female characters. Costumes, French, period 1661. Scenery, palace, gardens, prison. Can be arranged by amatuers but is a heavy piece. A fine leading man, heavy man, a glorious comedy, etc. Also leading lady, juvenile lady, comedy lady, etc. This drama was a favorite with Harold Forsberg. Time of performance, 2 hours and 15 minutes.

40. *THAT MYSTERIOUS BUNDLE.* A Farce in one act, by Hattie Lena Lambla. 2 male, 2 female characters. Costumes, modern. Scenery, a plain room. A Variety pcice, yet can be performed by Amatuers, etc. A Mysterious bundle figures in this farce, which contains a————. Time of performance, 20 minutes.

41. *WON AT LAST.* A Comedy Drama in 3 acts, by Wybert Reeve, 7 male, 3 female characters. Costumes modern. Scenery, drawing-room, street and office. Every character is good. Jennie Hight starred on the character of "Constance" in this play. Amatuers can produce it. Time of performance, 1 hour 45 minutes.

42. *DOMESTIC FELICITY.* A Farce in one act, by Hattie Lena Lambla, 1 male, 1 female character. Costumes modern. Scene, a dining room. The name fully describes the piece. Very funny. Time of performance, fifteen minutes.

43. *ARRAH DE BAUGH.* A Drama in 5 acts, by F. C. Kinnaman, 7 male, 5 female characters. Costumes modern. Scenes, exteriors and interiors. A most exquisite love story in a play, abounding in scenes of great beauty. The depth of woman's love is beautifully shown. Time of performance about two hours.

44. *OBEDIENCE, OR TOO MINDFUL BY FAR.* A Comedietta in one act, by Hattie Lena Lambla, 1 male, 2 female characters. Costumes modern. Scenes, plain room and bed room. An old fellow who thinks he is very sick, becomes vely peevish and particular. A plot is formed to break him of his foolishness. Very amusing. Time of performance twenty minutes.

45. *ROCK ALLEN THE ORPHAN, OR LOST AND FOUND.* A Comedy Drama in one act, by W. Henri Wilkins, 5 male, 3 female characters. Costumes modern. Scenes interiors. Time, during the Rebellion. This play represents the real "deown east" characters to perfection. An old man and woman are always quarreling, and their difficulties are very amusing. Time of performance, one hour and twenty minutes.

46. *MAN AND WIFE.* A Drama in five acts, by H. A. Webber, 12 male, 7 female characters. Costumes modern. Scenery exteriors and interiors. This drama is one of intense interest and is a faithful dramatization of Wilkie Collins' story of the same name. This is said by competant critics to be the best dramatization published, and it should be in the hands of every dramatic company in the country. It has become a great favorite.

47. *IN THE WRONG BOX.* An Ethiopean Farce in one act, by M. A. D. Clifton, 3 male characters. Costumes, peddler's and darkey's dilapidated dress. Scene, a wood. Characters represented, a darkey, an Irishman and a Yankee. Time of performance twenty minutes.

48. *SCHNAPPS.* A Dutch Farce in one act, M. A. D. Clifton, 1 male, 1 female character. Costumes, burlesque German. Scene, a plain room. A neat little piece for two Dutch players, introducing songs and dances. Time of performance, 15 to 30 minutes, at the pleasure of the performers

49. *DER TWO SUBPRISES.* A Dutch Farce in one act, by M. A. D. Clifton, 1 male, 1 female character. Costumes, peasant's, and old man's and old woman's dress. Scene, a kitchen. A very neat little sketch, introducing songs and dances. Time of performance, about twenty minutes.

50. *HAMLET.* A Tragedy in five acts, by Shakespeare, 15 male, 3 female characters. Probably no other play by the immortal Shakespeare is produced as frequently as this one. It needs no description. Time of performance about two hours and thirty minutes.

51. *RESCUED.* A Temperance Drama in two acts, by Clayton H. Gilbert, 5 male, 3 female characters. This play visibly depicts the dangerous consequences of falling into bad company, the follies of the intoxicating bowl, and shows that even the pure love of a noble girl will be sacrificed to the accursed appetite. The solemn scenes are balanced by the funny portions, and all in all the play is a grand success. Costumes modern. Scenes, interiors some neatly and some handsomely furnished. Time of performance one hour.

52. *HENRY GRANDEN.* A Drama in three acts, by Frank Lester Bingham, 11 male, 8 female characters. This drama is sensational in a high degree, abounding in thrilling scenes among the Indians, hair breadth escapes, etc. It should be purchased by every dramatic company that wish something to suit the public. Costumes not hard to arrange. Time of performance two hours.

53. *OUT IN THE STREETS.* A Temperance Drama in three acts, by S. N. Cook, 6 male, 4 female characters. Wherever this drama has been produced it has been received with the greatest enthusiasm. Listeners have been melted to tears at the troubles of Mrs. Bradford, and in the next scene been convulsed with laughter at the drolleries of North Carolina Pete. Costumes modern. Scenes, interiors. Time of performance, about one hour.

54. *THE TWO T. J's.* A Farce in one act, by Martin Beecher, 4 male, 2 female characters. Costumes of the day ; scene an ordinary room. This is a capital farce and has two male characters excellent for light and low comedians. Good parts also for old and young lady. Time of performance thirty minutes.

55. *SOMEBODY'S NOBODY.* A Farce in one act and one scene, by C. A. Maltby, 3 male, 2 female characters. Scene, interior. Easily arranged in any parlor or hall, as it can be produced without scenery. Costumes modern with the exception of Dick Mizzle's which is hostler's and afterwards extravagant fashionable. This most laughable farce was first produced at the Drury Lane Theater, London, where it had a run of one hundred and fifty consecutive nights. It is all comic, and has excellent parts for old man, walking gent, low comedy, walking lady and chambermaid. Time of performance, 30 minutes.

56. *WOOING UNDER DIFFICULTIES.* A Farce in one act and one scene, by John T. Douglass, 4 male, 3 female characters. Scene, handsomely furnished apartment. Costumes of the day. Probably no poor fellow ever wooed under more distressing difficulties than the one in this farce. It all comes about through a serious misunderstanding. A crusty old man, and a quarrelsome and very important servant go to make the farce extremely funny. Time of performance thirty minutes.

57. *PADDY MILES' BOY.* An Irish Farce in one act, by James Pilgrim, 5 male, 2 female characters. Scenes, exteriors and interiors. Costumes eccentric, and Irish for Paddy. Probably there is not an Irish farce published so often presented as this one, but it is always a favorite and is always received with great applause. Time of performance 35 minutes.

58. *WRECKED.* A Temperance play in two acts, by A. D. Ames, 9 male, 3 female characters. Scenes, drawing room, saloon, street and jail. Costumes modern. The lessons learned in this drama are most excellent. The language is pure, containing nothing to offend the most refined ear. From the comfortable home and pleasant fireside, it follows the downward course of the drunkard to the end. All this is followed by counterfeiting, the death of the faithful wife caused by a blow from the hand of a drunken husband, and finally the death of the drunkard in the madhouse. Time of performance about one hour.

59. *SAVED.* A Temperance Sketch in two acts, by Edwin Tardy, 2 male, 3 female characters. Scenes, street and plain room. Nicely adapted to amatuers, Time of performance twenty minutes.

60. *DRIVEN TO THE WALL, OR TRUE TO THE LAST.* A Play in four acts, by A. D. Ames. 10 male and 3 female characters. For beauty of dialogue, startling situations, depths of feeling, there is none on the American Stage superior to this one. The plot is an exceedingly deep one, and the interest begins with the first speech, and does not for a moment cease until the curtain falls on the last scene of the last act. The cast is small and the costumes easily arranged. It can be played on any stage. It has parts for Leading Emotional Lady, Juvenile Lady, Leading Man, Villain, Character Old Man. First Old Man, Comedy, etc.

61. *NOT AS DEAF AS HE SEEMS.* An Ethiopean Farce in one act. 2 male characters. Scene, a plain room. Costumes exagerated and comic. Extremely ridiculous and funny. Time of performance 15 minutes.

62. *TEN NIGHTS IN A BAR-ROOM.* A Temperance Play in five acts, by Wm. W. Pratt, from T. S. Arther's novel of the same name—7 male, 3 female characters. This edition is rewritten, containing many new points, and is the best ever presented to the public. Nothing need be said in its praise, as it is too well known. It is often played, and always successfully. Time of performance about two hours.

63. *THREE GLASSES A DAY,* Or, The Broken Home. A grand Moral and Temperance Drama, in two acts, by W. Henri Wilkins, 4 male, 2 female characters. Costumes modern. Scenes, interiors. First-class characters for Leading Man, Villain, a genuine down-east Yankee, which is also very funny ; also Leading Lady, and a tip-top Comedy Lady. If a company wishes something with an excellent moral, at the same time running over with genuine humor, buy this. Time of performance about one hour and thirty minutes.

64. *THAT BOY SAM.* An Ethiopean Farce in one act, by F. L. Cutler. 3 male, 1 female character. Scene, a plain room and common furniture. Costumes, comic, to suit the characters. Very funny, and effectually gives the troubles of a "colored gal" in trying to have a beau, and the pranks of "that boy Sam." Time of performance twenty minutes.

65. *AN UNWELCOME RETURN.* A Comic Interlude, in one act, by Geo. A. Munson. 3 male, 1 female character. Scene, a dining room. Costumes, modern. Companies will find this a very amusing piece, two negroes being very funny—enough so to keep an audience in the best of humor. Time of performance, twenty minutes.

66. *HANS, THE DUTCH J.* P. A Dutch Farce in one act, by F. L. Cutler, . 3 male, 1 female character. An exceedingly funny piece. Hans figures as a Justice in the absence of his master, and his exploits are extremely ludricous. Costumes modern. Scene, plain room. Time of performance, twenty minutes.

67. *THE FALSE FRIEND.* A Drama in two acts, by Geo. S. Vautrot. 6 male, 1 female character. Simple scenery and costumes. First class characters for leading man, old man, villain, a rollicking Irishman, etc. also a good leading lady. This drama is one of thrilling interest, and dramatic companies will invariably be pleased with it. Time of performance, one hour and forty-five minutes.

68. *THE SHAM PROFESSOR.* A Farce in one act, by F. L. Cutler. 4 male characters. This intensely funny afterpiece can be produced by any company. The characters are all first class, and the "colored individual" is especially funny. Scene, a plain room. Costumes, simple. Time of performance, about twenty minutes.

69. *MOTHER'S FOOL.* A Farce in one act, by W. Henri Wilkins. 6 male, 1 female character. Like all of Mr. Wilkins' plays, this is first class. The characters are all well drawn, it is very amusing, and proves an immense success wherever produced. Scene, a simple room. Costumes modern. Time of performance, thirty minutes.

70. *WHICH WILL HE MARRY.* A Farce in one act, by Thomas Egerton Wilks. 2 male, 8 female characters. Scene, a street. Costumes modern. Easily arranged on any stage. A barber hears that one of eight women has fallen heir to some money, not knowing which, he makes love to them all. This, together with the revenge the females have upon him, will prove laughable enough to suit any one. Time of representation, thirty minutes.

71. *THE REWARD OF CRIME, OR THE LOVE OF GOLD.* A Drama of Vermont, in two acts, by W. Henri Wilkins. 5 male, 3 female characters. A drama from the pen of this author is sufficient guarantee of its excellence. Characters for old man, 1st and 2d heavy men, juvenile. A splendid Yankee, lively enough to suit any one. Old woman, juvenile woman, and comedy. Costumes modern. Scene, plain rooms and street. Time of performance, one hour and thirty minutes. Easily placed upon the stage, and a great favorite with amatuers.

72. *THE DEUCE IS IN HIM.* A Farce in one act, by R. J. Raymond. 5 male, 1 female character. Scene, a plain room. Costumes modern. This farce is easily arranged, and can be produced on any stage, in fact, in a parlor. The pranks of the doctor's boy will keep an audience in roars of laughter, every line being full of fun. Time of performance, thirty minutes. Order this, and you will be pleased.

73. *AT LAST.* A Temperance Drama in three acts, by G. S. Vautrot. 7 male 1 female character. This is one of the most effective temperance plays ever published. Good characters for leading man, 1st and 2d villain, a detective, old man, a Yankee, and a capital negro, also leading lady. The temptations of city life are faithfully depicted, the effects of gambling, strong drink, etc. Every company that orders it will produce it. Costumes modern. Scene, Mobile, Time of performance, one hour and thirty minutes.

74. *HOW TO TAME YOUR MOTHER-IN-LAW.* A Farce in one act, by Henry J. Byron. 4 male, 2 female characters. Scene, parlor, supposed to be in the rear of a grocers shop. Costumes modern. Whiffles the proprietor of the grocery, has a mother-in-law who is always interfering with his business. Various expedients are resorted to to cure her—a mutual friend is called in. who, by the aid of various disguises frightens the old lady nearly to death, finally Whiffles gets on a "ge-lorious drunk," and at last triumphs. A perfect success. Time of performance, thirty-five minutes.

by A. D. Ames, 8 male, and 3 female characters. A thrilling drama,
favorite. Leading man, villian, two comedies, old man, leading lady
lady, etc. Costumes modern. The situations in this play, are most excelle
Time of performance, 1 hour and a half.

CPSIA information can be obtained
at www.ICGtesting.com
Printed in the USA
BVHW090230111218
535228BV00034B/2218/P